GOBI DESERT

INNER MONGOLIA
AUTONOMOUS REGION

HEILONGJIANG

JILIN

LIAONING

NORTH
KOREA

SOUTH
KOREA

Sea of
Japan
(East Sea)

JAPAN

BEIJING
● BEIJING

Tianjin ●
TIANJIN

Bohai
Sea

NGXIA HUI
UTONOMOUS
REGION

HEBEI

SHANXI

SHANDONG

Yellow
Sea

Yellow
River

SHAANXI

Xi'an ●

HENAN

JIANGSU

East
China
Sea

N

ANHUI

Nanjing ● Shanghai
SHANGHAI

HUBEI

Wuhan ●

Langtze River

CHONGQING

ZHEJIANG

HUNAN

JIANGXI

GUIZHOU

FUJIAN

Taipei

Tropic of Cancer

TAIWAN

GUANGDONG

Guangzhou ●

PACIFIC OCEAN

Pearl River

GUANGXI ZHUANG
AUTONOMOUS
REGION

● Hong Kong
HONG KONG SPECIAL
ADMINISTRATIVE REGION

MACAU SPECIAL
ADMINISTRATIVE REGION

IETNAM

Gulf of
Tonkin

HAINAN

South
China
Sea

PHILIPPINES

0   290   580   870 kilometres
Scale

D1358391

First published in 2008 by
MACMILLAN EDUCATION AUSTRALIA PTY LTD
15–19 Claremont Street, South Yarra 3141
Reprinted 2008

Visit our website at www.macmillan.com.au or go directly to www.macmillanlibrary.com.au

Associated companies and representatives throughout the world.

Copyright © John and Jackie Tidey 2008

All rights reserved.
Except under the conditions described in the *Copyright Act 1968* of Australia
and subsequent amendments, no part of this publication may be reproduced,
stored in a retrieval system, or transmitted in any form or by any means,
electronic, mechanical, photocopying, recording or otherwise, without the
prior written permission of the copyright owner.

Educational institutions copying any part of this book for educational purposes
under the Act must be covered by a Copyright Agency Limited (CAL) licence
for educational institutions and must have given a remuneration notice to CAL.
Licence restrictions must be adhered to. Any copies must be photocopies only,
and they must not be hired out or sold. For details of the CAL licence contact:
Copyright Agency Limited, Level 15, 233 Castlereagh Street, Sydney, NSW 2000.
Telephone: (02) 9394 7600. Facsimile: (02) 9394 7601. Email: info@copyright.com.au

National Library of Australia
Cataloguing-in-Publication data

Tidey, John.
  History and government.

  Includes index.
  For primary school children.
  ISBN 978 1 4202 2459 7 (hbk.).

  1. China – Juvenile literature. I. Tidey, Jackie. II. History and Government.
  (Series: Tidey, John. China: land, life and culture).

951

Edited by Georgina Garner
Text and cover design by Peter Shaw
Page layout by Peter Shaw
Photo research by Jes Senbergs
Maps by Damien Demaj, DEMAP

Printed in Hong Kong

Acknowledgements
The author and the publisher are grateful to the following for permission to reproduce copyright material:

Cover photograph: Tiananmen Square decorated with flowers for National Day, by James Wu

AAP Image/AP Photo/Ng Han Guan, 11; AusAID, 23 (top); Australia–China Council, 28 (all); BigstockPhoto, 25 (left);
Marion Ducco, 4 (top right); DW Stock Picture Library, 9; Getty Images, 6 (bottom right), 7, 12 (top), 13 (top), 14 (bottom),
16 (left & right), 20, 22 (top), 23 (middle & bottom); Alex Headley, 17 (top); © istockphoto.com, 4 (bottom left); © Ying
Chen/istockphoto.com, 4 (bottom right); © Robert Churchill/istockphoto.com, 3 (top right), 15; © Christine Gonslaves/
istockphoto.com, 6 (top right); © Bill Grove/istockphoto.com, 5 (bottom); © Alan Tobey/istockphoto.com, 10 (bottom);
© Gautier Willaume/istockphoto.com, 3 (top left), 8 (bottom); © Lisa Young/istockphoto.com, 25 (bottom); Lonely Planet
Images/Greg Elms, 14 (top), 17 (bottom); Melbourne Office Tianjin, 3 (bottom left), 29 (all); © Shutterstock, 25 (right);
© Norman Chan/Shutterstock, 19 (bottom); © Max FX/Shutterstock, 4 (bottom middle); © Edward Hor/Shutterstock,
10 (top); © Colin & Linda McKie/Shutterstock, 24; © Holger Mette/Shutterstock, 18; © Taol Mor/Shutterstock, 19 (top);
© Hu Xiao Fang/Shutterstock, 6 (bottom left); Jackie Tidey, 21 (top); Wikipedia Images, 6 (top left), 12 (bottom); Weidong
Yang, 21 (bottom); James Wu, 1, 4 (top left & top middle), 5 (top), 8 (top), 13 (bottom), 22 (middle & bottom), 26, 27.

While every care has been taken to trace and acknowledge copyright, the publisher tenders their apologies for any accidental
infringement where copyright has proved untraceable. Where the attempt has been unsuccessful, the publisher welcomes
information that would redress the situation.

Contents

China, a big country   4

China's recent past   5

China's long history   6

Ancient China   8

The early empire   10

The second empire   12

The birth of modern China   14

The People's Republic of China   16

How China is governed   18

China and the media   20

China's economy   22

International trade   24

China's National Day   26

Embassies and consulates   27

working together   28

A great power once again   30

Glossary   31

Index   32

Glossary Words

When a word is printed in **bold**, you can look up its meaning in the Glossary on page 31.

Chinese proverb

To know the road ahead, ask those who are coming back

China, a big country

China challenges the imagination because of its size. It is big in many ways. It is one of the largest countries on Earth, covering about one-fifth of the continent of Asia. China's population of more than 1.3 billion, or 1 300 000 000, is the world's largest. It has an ancient civilisation and a recorded history that date back thousands of years.

A large area of China is covered by tall mountains and wide deserts. Most of the population live in the fertile lowlands that are bordered by the Pacific Ocean in the east.

The People's Republic of China

Today, China is formally known as the People's Republic of China (PRC). In the last 30 years, the PRC has gone through great social change and the **economy** has grown enormously. China is now one of Australia's major trading partners.

This book explores China's long and eventful history. It looks at how China is governed today as one of the world's great powers. It also explores how Chinese and Australians are working together to exchange ideas and build international relationships.

An ancient history

Traditional arts

Very old customs

A country of extremes

A rich variety of wildlife

Plants and traditional medicines

China's recent past

The People's Republic of China (PRC) is governed by the Chinese Communist Party. China is on the way to becoming the most powerful country on Earth.

It was not always like this. For thousands of years, China was ruled by kings, emperors and their dynasties. Ordinary people worked hard, but most were poor farmers or traders. Nearly 100 years ago, the last of the **empires** collapsed, and China became a republic. The country went through almost four decades of turmoil and **civil war**. Eventually, the **communist forces** were successful and established the PRC in 1949.

In recent times, China has made great advances in many areas. These advances include a raised **standard of living** for most of the population, and the development of major modern cities, such as Shanghai, Beijing and Guangzhou. Other advances in the last 30 years are the growth in manufacturing industries, increased trade with other countries and improvements in agriculture and health.

For Your Information

In a model communist society, the people own everything and the government pays them wages according to their needs.

Did You Know?

A **dynasty** is a series of rulers who belong to the same family.

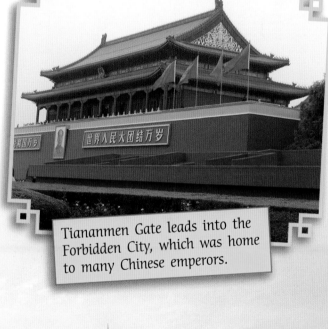

Tiananmen Gate leads into the Forbidden City, which was home to many Chinese emperors.

Some of the buildings in Shanghai look like they are from the future.

China's long history

China has a very long and rich history. Historians have identified four key periods of importance in China's history:

- ancient China (2200 BCE–221 BCE)
- the early empire (221 BCE–589 CE)
- the second empire (589 CE–1644 CE)
- modern China (1644 CE to the present)

Within each of these periods, there were many rulers and many dynasties.

For Your Information

Fossilised remains that date back more than 250 000 years were found in China in the early 1900s. They belong to Peking man (also called Beijing man), who was an early member of an extinct species of humans.

Ancient China

The early empire

The second empire

Modern China

From dynasty to republic

The rule of China has changed throughout history. Its government has ranged from ancient dynasties, to empires ruled by emperors, to a modern communist republic, the People's Republic of China.

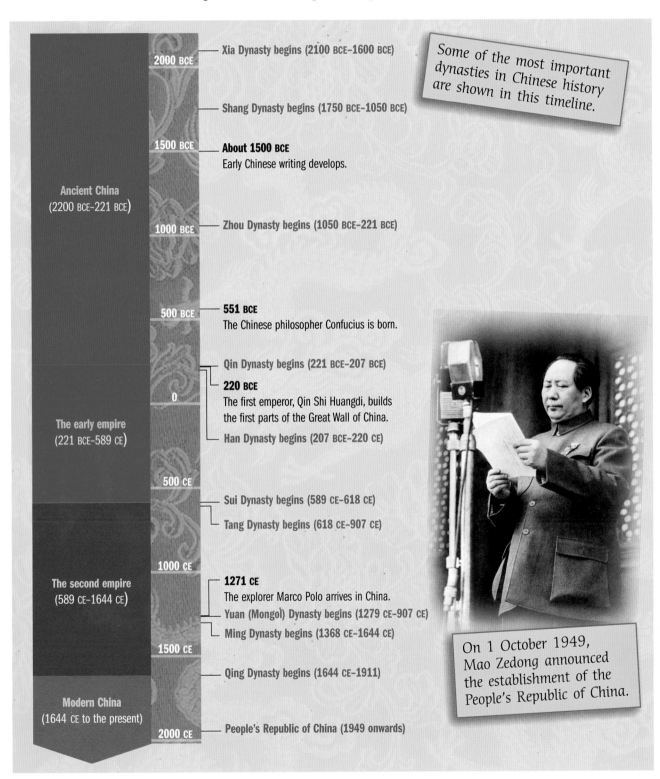

Some of the most important dynasties in Chinese history are shown in this timeline.

Ancient China
(2200 BCE–221 BCE)

The early empire
(221 BCE–589 CE)

The second empire
(589 CE–1644 CE)

Modern China
(1644 CE to the present)

2000 BCE — Xia Dynasty begins (2100 BCE–1600 BCE)

— Shang Dynasty begins (1750 BCE–1050 BCE)

1500 BCE — **About 1500 BCE**
Early Chinese writing develops.

1000 BCE — Zhou Dynasty begins (1050 BCE–221 BCE)

500 BCE — **551 BCE**
The Chinese philosopher Confucius is born.

— Qin Dynasty begins (221 BCE–207 BCE)
0 — **220 BCE**
The first emperor, Qin Shi Huangdi, builds the first parts of the Great Wall of China.
— Han Dynasty begins (207 BCE–220 CE)

500 CE — Sui Dynasty begins (589 CE–618 CE)
— Tang Dynasty begins (618 CE–907 CE)

1000 CE — **1271 CE**
The explorer Marco Polo arrives in China.
— Yuan (Mongol) Dynasty begins (1279 CE–907 CE)
— Ming Dynasty begins (1368 CE–1644 CE)

1500 CE — Qing Dynasty begins (1644 CE–1911)

2000 CE — People's Republic of China (1949 onwards)

On 1 October 1949, Mao Zedong announced the establishment of the People's Republic of China.

7

Ancient China

Before 2200 BCE, the land that is now China was inhabited by small groups of people living in tribes, farming the land. The first dynasty to unite a large area of China was called the Xia Dynasty. The Xia ruled an area north of the Yellow River. Not much is known about the Xia Dynasty.

The Shang Dynasty

The Shang Dynasty ruled from about 1750 BCE until 1050 BCE. The earliest and most complete record of Chinese writing that has been found comes from the Shang Dynasty. The Shang were also highly skilled at working in bronze.

The Zhou Dynasty

The long-running Zhou Dynasty introduced a golden age of new ideas and **philosophies**. The Zhou Dynasty ruled from around 1050 BCE until 221 BCE. **Legalism**, **Confucianism** and **Taoism**, which is sometimes called Daoism, gave people philosophical rules to live by.

This bronze vessel from the Shang Dynasty was used to hold food.

For Your Information

Chinese law developed from Confucianism and Legalism more than 2500 years ago. It is one of the oldest legal **traditions** in the world.

MEET Meet Confucius

Confucius, the famous Chinese thinker and philosopher, was born in the city of Qufu, in the Shandong Province, in 551 BCE. His teachings have been developed into a system of philosophy known as Confucianism. The teachings of Confucius are found in his sayings.

Confucius said, 'Silence is a friend who will never betray'. He also said, 'I hear and I forget. I see and I remember. I do and I understand.'

The Mandate of Heaven

The **doctrine** of *Tianming*, or the Mandate of Heaven, was developed during the Zhou Dynasty. Good things happen to rulers and their people if the rulers are honest, virtuous and just, according to this doctrine. The ruler has the Mandate of Heaven, or heaven's approval. Rulers lose their right to rule when they stop ruling fairly and justly. They have lost the mandate. It is taken away from them and passed to a new ruler who will be honest, virtuous and just. Sometimes the Mandate of Heaven was passed on through natural means, such as the death of a ruler, but at other times it was passed on by violent means.

A mandate for all

This idea of fairness and justice spread throughout Chinese society over time and was applied to everyone. It was the duty of every person to care for those they were related to. The Mandate of Heaven is an important social and political idea in Chinese culture.

Did You Know?

The Mandate of Heaven is similar to the European 'Divine Rights of Kings'. This idea approved of just rulers, and allowed unjust rulers to be overthrown.

Chinese people believe that they have a duty to look after their family members.

The early empire

For hundreds of years, many rulers in local areas in China fought each other for power and territory. In 221 BCE, the whole of China became united for the first time. This was the beginning of the remarkable Qin Dynasty. Qin Shi Huangdi became the first emperor of the united empire at 13 years of age. Before this time, rulers in China had called themselves kings.

For Your Information

Emperor Qin Shi Huangdi's name is made up of two parts:

- Qin, which is the name of his dynasty, or family
- Shi Huangdi, which translates as 'First Emperor'. *Huangdi* was a new Chinese word that translated as 'emperor'.

The first emperor

Emperor Qin Shi Huangdi is a major figure in the long history of China. It was Emperor Qin who ordered high, strong walls to be built in the north to keep out bands of invading warriors. In time, these walls were linked with others and became the Great Wall of China.

More than 8000 life-size **terracotta** figures of warriors and horses were buried with Qin Shi Huangdi in Xi'an when he died. This Terracotta Army was not discovered until 1974.

Only parts of the Terracotta Army have been uncovered from their clay tombs.

Each of the 8000 or more warriors has a different face.

The Han Dynasty

Soon after the Qin Dynasty collapsed, the Han Dynasty began. It lasted from 207 BCE until 220 CE. This dynasty went on to play a significant role in Chinese history.

Chinese scientists made the first magnetic compass during the Han Dynasty. They also invented the first simple seismograph to measure the severity of earthquakes. Paper was invented, and the first dictionary was produced at this time. This dynasty also saw advances in medicine.

Running ancient China and collecting taxes was difficult in such a large and, even then, heavily populated country. The Han developed an efficient system to run China. Every dynasty that followed them copied this system.

For Your Information

Ban Gu (32 CE–92 CE), with his father Ban Biao and his sister Ban Zhao, wrote an official history called *Hanshu* or *History of the former Han Dynasty*. This book took more than 80 years to write and had more than 100 chapters. It became the model for later Chinese historical writing.

Did You Know?

The main ethnic group in China today is called the Han, in honour of this dynasty of great achievement.

About nine out of ten modern Chinese are Han Chinese.

The second empire

The Chinese empire began to fall apart between the end of the Han Dynasty in 220 CE and the beginning of the Sui Dynasty in 589 CE. These years were marked by chaos, natural disasters and warfare. Under the Sui and the great Tang dynasties, the empire was reunited.

The Tang Dynasty

The Tang was the greatest dynasty of the second empire. It ruled from 618 CE until 907 CE. The Tang expanded the boundaries of China to the north, east and south. Empress Wu of the Tang Dynasty is the only woman to have borne the ruler's title in China's history.

For Your Information

When important people died during the Han and Tang dynasties, they were often buried with hundreds of pottery figurines. Sometimes these figurines were animals. Sometimes they represented the dead person's servants. When many of these tombs were **excavated** in the 1900s, these figurines were uncovered and placed in museums.

Life-size stone statues guard the tomb where the Tang Dynasty rulers Gao Zong and Wu Zetian were buried.

MEET Meet Empress Wu

Empress Wu was born in 624 CE to wealthy parents. She was the only woman to run China in its long history. She arranged the murders of rivals and even members of her own family during her ruthless rise to power in the Tang Dynasty.

Empress Wu was a capable leader and made many improvements, particularly in irrigation and farming. She has been called the most influential and mysterious woman in the history of China.

Mongol rule

In 1279 CE, the Mongols invaded China. The Mongol Empire had already conquered Europe and Asia, led by the famous warrior and horseman Genghis Khan. Genghis Khan's grandson, Kublai Khan, founded the Yuan, or Mongol, Dynasty in China. While the Yuan is called a dynasty, the rule by the Mongols was really a **government of occupation**. The Yuan Dynasty lasted about 90 years. It was the shortest of the major dynasties.

Did You Know?

Marco Polo (1254 CE–1324 CE) was an Italian voyager, merchant, explorer and writer. He travelled widely in China and had a brilliant career in the service of Kublai Khan.

The Ming Dynasty

The Ming Dynasty followed the Yuan Dynasty and lasted from 1368 CE until 1644 CE. This dynasty was founded by a peasant, who led a peasants' revolt against the Mongols. The Ming Dynasty was a creative and prosperous time in China. One of the great cultural developments of this dynasty was the development of the novel. Some of the best known works from the Ming period are still read in China today.

For Your Information

Zheng He, also called Cheng Ho, was probably China's most famous navigator. During the Ming Dynasty, Zheng He made several long voyages, visiting more than 30 countries. He is thought to have sailed around south-east Asia, India and eastern Africa. Some people think that he also sailed to North America and South America.

Huge statues of warriors line the path leading to the Ming emperors' tombs near Beijing.

Did You Know?

The founder of the Ming Dynasty reinforced the Great Wall to keep out the Mongols from the north. The Great Wall, as it is today, is largely a Ming structure.

The birth of modern China

China's last dynasty, the Qing Dynasty, marks the birth of modern China. It began in 1644 when the Manchus took over the country and founded the Qing Dynasty.

The Qing Dynasty

The Manchus were originally from tribes in Manchuria, in north-eastern China. During their long time in power, they became inward-looking and inflexible rulers. They did not think other countries were equal to China. This affected their trade and dealings with the rest of the world. In 1911, the Qing Dynasty collapsed. The dynastic system of rule in China had ended.

For Your Information

The Qing Dynasty fought many losing battles against **Western** influence on Chinese culture. Between 1839 and 1842, it fought against the importing of opium into China by Britain. At the end of the war, China was forced to surrender the island of Hong Kong to the British.

These portraits are of a high official and his wife from the Qing Dynasty.

MEET Meet Pu Yi

Pu Yi was the child emperor of the Qing Dynasty. He was the last emperor of China. Pu Yi was made emperor before his third birthday. He gave up his throne at the age of 5. Pu Yi died in 1967 after many hardships and adventures. He wrote about these in his book, *From Emperor to Citizen*.

A new republic

A Chinese republic was established after the end of the Qing Dynasty. Instead of an emperor or king, there was a president.

Sun Yat-sen became the new republic's president. When he died in 1925, a long civil war began. Sun Yat-sen's Chinese Nationalist Party, called the *Kuomintang*, and the Communist Party of China both struggled for control of China. This struggle continued for more than 20 years.

In 1949, the Communist Party, led by Mao Zedong, triumphed. The People's Republic of China was established. A new era had begun in China.

China's flag

In 1949, citizens were invited to submit designs for a new flag. Almost 3000 were received. The chosen flag was flown officially for the first time in Beijing's Tiananmen Square on 1 October 1949, the day the People's Republic of China was founded.

The Chinese flag is bright red all over, representing the spirit of the communist revolution. In its top-left corner, there is one large and four small yellow stars. The small stars represent the people under the leadership of the Communist Party of China.

Did You Know?

China's first national flag featured a blue dragon reaching for the red Sun. Before 1872, there was no national flag.

The large star on China's flag is said to represent the Communist Party.

The People's Republic of China

In 1949, when the People's Republic of China was founded, Mao Zedong's new government introduced tough controls on Chinese society and its economy. Mao Zedong cut off contact with most other countries.

In the years that followed, the Chinese people experienced great changes and many hardships. Many millions of people died of starvation. China was virtually closed to the outside world for nearly 30 years. A 'bamboo curtain' came down, and other countries knew little of what was happening there.

The Cultural Revolution

One of Mao Zedong's experiments in change was the Cultural Revolution. Students were encouraged by the government to question all authority, even their parents and teachers. Educated people, such as doctors, scientists and academics, were sent to work as labourers on farms. Historic buildings and artefacts were deliberately destroyed. The Cultural Revolution caused enormous upheaval and chaos throughout China.

During the Cultural Revolution, huge numbers of young people gathered, chanting slogans and questioning those in authority.

Red Guards chanted slogans from Mao Zedong's *Little Red Book*.

Did You Know?

Sayings and quotations by Mao Zedong were published in 1964 in the *Little Red Book*, as it is called in the West. More than 900 million copies of Mao's book have been printed.

Meet Mao Zedong

Chairman Mao, sometimes called 'the great helmsman', was China's leader from 1949 until his death in 1976. He was a complex man. He was a soldier, statesman, thinker, writer and a hero to many, and yet he was a tyrant in many ways.

Mao was born in 1893 into a family of well-off peasants in the south of China. He joined the Chinese Communist Party and became head of the party in 1943.

When Mao first came to power as leader of the People's Republic of China, he achieved a great deal. The Communists set about reorganising and rebuilding the country. China had been badly damaged by a war with Japan, as well as by a long-running civil war.

Mao was closely associated with two great human and social disasters. The Great Leap Forward program of 1958 and the Cultural Revolution from 1966 to 1976 cost millions of lives.

After Mao Zedong

In 1976, Mao Zedong died. In 1978, Deng Xiaoping emerged as China's leader. Deng realised that China needed to reconnect with the outside world. He introduced many economic changes that modernised the country and people began to visit China again.

Large posters helped persuade people that communist ideals were best.

How China is governed

China is governed by the Communist Party of China. All official key positions in the government are occupied by members of the Communist Party. The Communist Party itself is controlled by a small and powerful committee, called the **Politburo**.

Communist government

The three main parts of China's government are:
- the President
- the National People's Congress
- the State Council.

The President of the People's Republic of China is the country's head of state and also the supreme representative of China at home and abroad.

The National People's Congress is like a national parliament elected by Chinese voters. It is made up of about 3000 people.

The State Council is made up of about 50 people, including the Premier, Vice-Premiers and other senior people in government, such as those in charge of government departments. The State Council puts in place the regulations and laws that are made by the National People's Congress. It also has the job of carrying out the policies of the Communist Party.

Local-level government

The central government in Beijing does not always control what goes on at a local level in the provinces of China. There are local or regional governments for:
- more than 20 provinces
- five autonomous regions
- four municipalities, which are under the control of the central government in Beijing
- two Special Administrative Regions (SARs), which are Macau and Hong Kong.

For Your Information

China's system of government is single-party rule. This means that only one political party is allowed to rule. Some other countries under single-party rule are:
- North Korea
- Cuba
- Vietnam
- Laos.

Government buildings in Tiananmen Square, in Beijing, have armed Chinese guards.

Macau

Macau is a small territory on the southern coast of China. In 1999, it became a SAR. Before then it was governed by the Portuguese for more than 400 years.

Hong Kong

Hong Kong is on the southern coast of China not far from Macau. In 1997, it became a SAR. Part of what is now called Hong Kong was once a British colony.

Hong Kong means 'fragrant harbour'. Hong Kong has long been seen as a busy place where the East meets the West. As one of the new Special Administrative Regions, Hong Kong will have a large amount of **autonomy** until 2047. It has its own currency and legal system, as well as freedom of the media and freedom to practise all religions. China is responsible for Hong Kong's military and diplomatic matters.

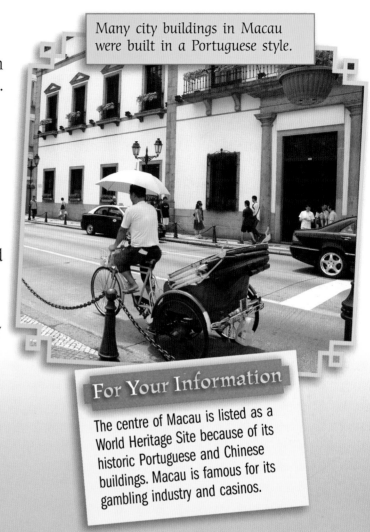

Many city buildings in Macau were built in a Portuguese style.

For Your Information

The centre of Macau is listed as a World Heritage Site because of its historic Portuguese and Chinese buildings. Macau is famous for its gambling industry and casinos.

The view from Victoria Peak on Hong Kong Island is of tall buildings, Victoria Harbour and Kowloon Peninsula.

China and the media

The Chinese government tries to control newspapers, television, Internet and radio so that it controls what people read, see and hear. The media in China is not free to publish and report on everything that is news. Chinese people cannot access many foreign websites on the Internet. However, this is changing. There are many new newspapers and magazines that discuss crime, consumer issues and other social issues.

Did You Know?

The Xinhua news agency was set up in 1931. It was originally called the Red China News Agency.

There are many new magazines and newspapers in China.

Government-owned media

Some of the largest media organisations in China are government agencies. These include:
- the China Central Television Network (CCTV), which is a government agency that claims an audience of more than one billion people
- Xinhua news agency, which is a very large organisation that distributes news within China and overseas
- the *People's Daily*, which is the official newspaper of the Communist Party of China.

China Daily

Overseas journalists played a major role in setting up the English-language newspaper *China Daily*, which is sometimes called the 'window to China'. The *China Daily* is owned by the government. It is the only national, English-language, daily newspaper in China.

For Your Information

The *China Youth Daily* was established in 1951 and is run by the Communist Youth League of China. It is the first profit-making, official, daily newspaper in China.

The number of *China Daily* newspapers sold in China grows as the number of English-speakers and tourists grows.

MEET Meet Weidong Yang

Weidong Yang is a young reporter from Henan Province, in central China. He studied journalism in Beijing at a school run by Xinhua news agency. Australian and American journalists taught international journalism subjects to the Chinese students at the school.

In conversation with Weidong Yang

I now work in Beijing as a business news reporter with *Asia Economic Weekly*.
After graduating from university my major studies in international journalism helped me get a job as a reporter. My main interests are business news and international news and I particularly enjoy the fact that my work exposes me to developments in China and abroad. *Asia Economic Weekly* is published in Chinese and English.

China's economy

Although China is still a developing country, it is in fact the world's fastest growing major economy. In recent decades, China's economy has grown quickly. It has grown an average of 9.5 per cent a year.

In 1978, under the leadership of Deng Xiaoping, China began opening up to the world. Deng began to allow trade and travel between China and other countries. Since then, the country has been transformed. It was once a mainly rural economy, with large numbers of poor people. It is now a place where many people work in industry, such as in factories, as well as in farming. Economic growth has lifted people's incomes and it has reduced poverty. But the growth has been uneven. Cities on the coast have experienced the most economic development and benefits. Rural areas have developed least.

Chinese workers in a Beijing factory make mascots for the 2008 Olympic Games.

A small business may be a meat stall in a city backstreet.

Less government regulation

Changes by the central government have meant that many businesses are now privately owned and the price of goods is no longer fixed by the government. Most new jobs are created by fast-growing private businesses. There have been a large number of job losses in government-owned businesses. This is because the government has changed the structure of businesses to make them more competitive.

A stallholder sells live eels, fish and other wildlife at a street market in Shanghai.

Did You Know?
By 2006, there were more than 25 million small businesses registered in China.

China's agriculture

Agricultural jobs are by far the main occupations in China. Most agricultural production is in the east of the country. China is the world's biggest producer of rice and wheat. It also produces the most cotton, tobacco and red meat, including beef, veal, mutton and lamb.

Rice has been grown in China for more than 9000 years.

China's industries

China has many large industries, such as those that produce energy, chemicals, machinery, iron and steel. Many types of industries rely on the manufacture of goods. These goods range from food and sporting goods to toys, electrical appliances and wooden products. Manufacturing is regarded as one of the pillars, or most important industries, of the Chinese economy.

For Your Information

Even though China is the world's biggest producer of rice, it does not produce enough rice to supply its large population. It imports rice from other countries, such as:

- Thailand
- Vietnam
- Japan
- Myanmar (Burma)
- Italy.

China's mining industry

China has a large mining industry. It ranks first in the world in coal production. It also has large iron ore deposits and is a major oil producer. China exports minerals such as tungsten, tin and mercury. It is one of the world's largest producers of aluminium.

Many electrical appliances, such as microwaves, are made and sold in China.

Coal is produced from many mines, large and small, in China.

International trade

China has become one of the top trading nations in the world because it buys and sells many goods. This trade has a major impact on the world's economy.

Trading with China

China has become a very important trading partner for many countries. About 40 per cent of the goods and services produced in China in 2006 were exported, or sold to other countries. One-fifth of this is sold to the United States, which is China's major trading partner. China sells manufactured goods, such as clothing, computers, machinery, plastics, iron and steel, to other countries. Look for the 'Made in China' tag on some of your toys and clothes. China buys goods such as natural gas, iron ore, coal, copper, sugar and wool from other countries.

Did You Know?

When doing business, the relationship between buyer and seller, called *guangxi*, is important. It is more important than offering a low price. Chinese people value others' courtesy and respect for their customs.

For Your Information

In 2006, China replaced the United States as the world's largest exporter of information and communications technology goods, such as digital cameras and mobile phones.

Containers are unloaded from a ship in Victoria Harbour, in Hong Kong.

Did You Know?

In 2004, more than 41 800 000 international tourists visited China.

China's currency

Chinese money is called *renminbi* (RMB), which means 'the people's currency'. There are a lot of notes and coins in Chinese currency. Chinese money is issued by the People's Bank of China. This bank is run by the People's Republic of China. The first *renminbi* banknotes were introduced during the civil war in 1948, before the founding of the People's Republic of China.

Did You Know?

The word *yuan* means round in Chinese. Ancient Chinese coins were round and also called *yuan*.

Chinese money

Yuan

The main unit of *renminbi* is the *yuan*. The *yuan* comes in 1, 2, 5, 10, 20, 50 and 100 *yuan* paper notes. There is also a 1 *yuan* coin.

Jiao

Smaller values of notes are called *jiao*. There are ten *jiao* to one *yuan*. The *jiao* comes in 1, 2 and 5 *jiao* paper notes. There are also 1 *jiao* and 5 *jiao* coins.

Fen

The smallest unit of currency is the *fen*. There are ten *fen* to one *jiao*. The *fen* comes in 1, 2 and 5 *fen* coins.

1 *yuan* coins

1 *fen* coin

5 *fen* coin

China's National Day

China's National Day is 1 October. It is celebrated as a public holiday throughout the People's Republic of China (PRC). It marks the day in 1949 when the PRC was established. This day ended years of civil war in China.

Celebrations on National Day include fireworks, concerts and parades. The celebrations take place around the nation. Public places, such as Beijing's historic Tiananmen Square, are decorated for the occasion. Around the world, Chinese embassies and consulates invite visitors to celebrate the PRC's National Day.

For Your Information

Tiananmen Square is a large public square in the heart of Beijing, the capital city of China. Tiananmen means *Gate of Heavenly Peace*, and the square dates back to the early 1400s. The PRC was proclaimed in Tiananmen Square on 1 October 1949 by Mao Zedong. The square was also the setting for protests in 1919, 1976 and 1989.

Tiananmen Square, in Beijing, is decorated with red and yellow flowers for National Day.

Did You Know?

National Day on 1 October is the start of a seven-day national holiday, called a 'Golden Week'. China has three Golden Week holidays each year.

Embassies and consulates

Embassies and consulates are offices that countries, such as China, set up in another country, called the host country. Ambassadors and diplomats work in embassies and consulates. They represent the interests of their country when dealing with the host country.

The Australian Embassy in China is in Beijing.

Embassy and consulate help

Embassy and consulate workers deal with the host country and report back to their own country. They help travellers and business people from their own country by providing information about the host country. They also supply visas, which are passes that allow people to travel in other countries.

For Your Information

In 1972, Australia and the People's Republic of China established their formal diplomatic relation. At this time, the two countries exchanged ambassadors.

Ambassadors and diplomats

An ambassador is a person who lives and works in a host country. The ambassador is the main representative of the government in that country and is in charge of their country's embassy. Ambassadors have professional diplomats advising them and helping them do their job. Diplomats manage relations between peoples or countries.

CHINESE AND AUSTRALIANS

The Australia–China Council was established in 1972 to foster friendship between the people of Australia and China. Since then, it has encouraged and supported exchanges between both countries in the fields of arts, education and business.

Youth exchange

The Australia–China Council has set up youth exchange programs for students still in school, for those who have just completed secondary school and for university students and graduates. These exchanges have two main aims. One is to encourage young Australians to develop a life-long interest and involvement in Australia–China relations. The other is to develop a large group of young Australian graduates with Chinese language skills.

Year in China Program

The Year in China Program gives secondary school graduates who have done well in language studies an opportunity to attend university in China for a year. Costs such as airfares, tuition and accommodation are covered by the Australia–China Council.

Australia-China Council

Young Australians visit the Great Wall during their year in China.

Many strong Chinese-Australian relationships are formed by people in the Year in China Program.

Sister cities

Melbourne and Tianjin are sister cities. This special relationship was established in 1980. It was the first sister-city relationship between a city in Australia and one in the People's Republic of China (PRC). Tianjin is an historic port in the north of China and the third-largest city in the PRC. Melbourne has set up an office in Tianjin. Many events, partnerships and exchanges between the two cities have taken place in fields such as culture, business and education.

A tall television and radio tower dominates the skyline in Tianjin.

Representing two cities

Melbourne and Tianjin have a sister-cities logo. Tianjin is represented by a red Chinese rose. The rose symbolises peace, friendship, prosperity and development. Melbourne is represented by the golden leaf, which is adapted from the City of Melbourne logo. The golden leaf symbolises Melbourne's parks and gardens and its urban environment.

Melbourne Tianjin
Sister Cities
墨尔本天津
友好城市

Tianjin and Melbourne are both represented on their sister-cities logo.

Tianjin city representatives wear local football scarves at a Melbourne reception.

Did You Know?

The first Chinese-Australian Lord Mayor, Alec Fong Lim, was elected Lord Mayor of Darwin in 1984 and again in 1988.

A great power once again

China is one of the oldest civilisations on Earth. Many hundreds of years ago, it led the world in economic, scientific and cultural areas. Then, for a long time, it turned its back on the world and went through a time of war, famine and upheaval.

China is on the rise again as a great power. It has been less than 30 years since the People's Republic of China began to open up to the world. In that time, it has experienced great economic growth and social progress. China's rapid progress is having an impact on the whole world.

Australia's relationship with China

Australia seeks a constructive and friendly relationship with China. These two countries share many interests, but there are some differences too, particularly in the area of human rights. China and Australia are major trading partners and cooperate in many cultural, health-related, educational and business activities.

China's future

How might the People's Republic of China be governed in the future? We cannot know. Sooner or later, China's economic progress may pave the way for a more democratic China.

Did You Know?

The United Nations is a group of nations that promotes international peace and cooperation. The People's Republic of China has been a member of the United Nations since 1971.

The future of China is in the hands of its young people.

Glossary

autonomy	self-government
civil war	a war between groups of people within their own country
communist forces	the Communist Party of China, who believe all property is owned equally by everyone in a society
Confucianism	a system of philosophy developed by the Chinese writer Confucius (551 BCE–479 BCE)
doctrine	a body of teaching related to a particular subject
dynasty	a series of rulers who belong to the same family
economy	the finances of a country
empires	groups of nations or peoples ruled by emperors
excavated	to unearth or uncover by digging
government of occupation	people who have come from another country and taken control
Legalism	an ancient Chinese philosophy in which law is the supreme authority
philosophies	sets of beliefs based on the study of wisdom and knowledge
Politburo	the main policy-making committee of the Communist Party of China
standard of living	a measure of how well or how poorly people live in a country
Taoism	an ancient Chinese philosophy that focuses on *Dao*, or 'the way'
terracotta	hard, clay pottery
traditions	customs and beliefs that are handed down
Western	related to the parts of the world that are not covered by eastern Asia

Index

A
agriculture 5, 23
ambassadors 27
ancient China 6, 8

B
Beijing 5, 15, 18, 26
business 22, 27, 28, 29, 30

C
China Daily 21
Chinese law 8
civil war 5, 15, 17
Communist Party of China 5, 15, 17, 18
Communist Youth League of China 21
Confucianism 8
Confucius 7, 8
consulates 27
Cultural Revolution 16, 17
currency 25

D
Daoism 8
Deng Xiaoping 17, 22
diplomats 27
dynasties 5, 6, 7, 8, 9, 10, 11, 12, 13, 14

E
early empire 6, 7, 10–11
economy 16, 22–23, 30
embassies 27
emperors 5, 10, 14
Empress Wu 12

F
flag 15

G
Great Leap Forward 17
Great Wall of China 7, 10, 13

H
Han Dynasty 11, 12
Han people 11
health 5
history 4, 6–7, 8–9, 10–11, 12–13, 14–15, 16–17

I
industry 22, 23
international trade 24–25
Internet 20

L
last emperor 14
Legalism 8
Little Red Book 16
local-level government 18

M
Macau 18, 19
Manchuria 14
Manchus 14
Mandate of Heaven 9
manufacturing 5, 24
Mao Zedong 15, 16, 17, 26
Marco Polo 7, 13
media 20, 21
Ming Dynasty 13
mining 23
modern China 6, 7, 14–15
Mongols 13

N
National Day 26
National People's Congress 18

P
Peking man 6
People's Bank of China 25
People's Republic of China (PRC) 5, 7, 14, 15, 16, 17, 25, 26, 27, 29, 30
Politburo 18
Pu Yi 14

Q
Qin Dynasty 7, 10–11
Qing Dynasty 7, 14, 15
Qin Shi Huangdi 7, 10

R
regional government 18
republic 5, 15
rice 23

S
second empire 6, 7, 12–13
Shang Dynasty 7, 8
single-party rule 18
sister cities 29
small businesses 22
Special Administrative Regions (SARs) 18, 19
State Council 18
Sui Dynasty 12
Sun Yat-sen 14

T
Tang Dynasty 12
Taoism 8
Terracotta Army 10
Tiananmen Square 15, 18, 26
tombs 12, 13
tourism 24
trade 5, 24, 30

X
Xia Dynasty 8
Xi'an 10
Xinhua news agency 20, 21

Y
Yuan Dynasty 12

Z
Zhou Dynasty 7, 8, 9

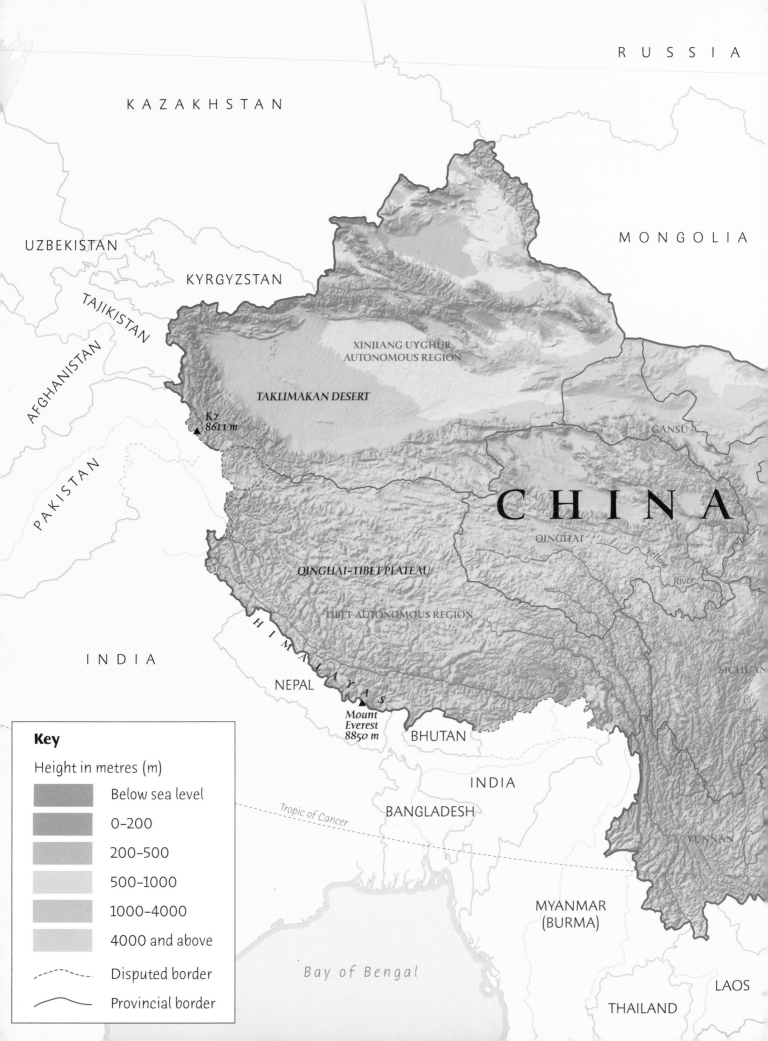

RUSSIA

KAZAKHSTAN

UZBEKISTAN

KYRGYZSTAN

TAJIKISTAN

AFGHANISTAN

PAKISTAN

MONGOLIA

XINJIANG UYGHUR
AUTONOMOUS REGION

TAKLIMAKAN DESERT

K2
8611 m

GANSU

CHINA

QINGHAI

Yellow
River

QINGHAI-TIBET PLATEAU

TIBET AUTONOMOUS REGION

SICHUAN

H
I
M
A
L
A
Y
A
S

INDIA

NEPAL

Mount
Everest
8850 m

BHUTAN

INDIA

YUNNAN

BANGLADESH

Tropic of Cancer

LAOS

MYANMAR
(BURMA)

Bay of Bengal

THAILAND

Key

Height in metres (m)

Below sea level

0–200

200–500

500–1000

1000–4000

4000 and above

- - - Disputed border

Provincial border